I WANT TO BE A
FASHION DESIGNER

Written by
Jocelyn Chua

Edited by
Jonathan Reule

Illustration
Carlos Varejão

Storyboard
Keziah Gan & Christiane Tee

Copyright © 2023 by Unibino Pte. Ltd.

First paperback edition October 2023
ISBN 978-981-17359-2-9

Published by Unibino Pte. Ltd.
9 North Buona Vista Drive, #02-01 Metropolis Tower 1, Singapore 138588

www.unibino.com

Have you ever wondered how the first piece of clothing in the world came to be? Who designed some of the earliest outfits and accessories during ancient times? And what were some of the purposes and functions of these forms of attire created by our ancestors over the ages?

If you have ever wondered about these things or dreamt of creating your own unique line of clothing, shoes, and accessories for yourself or your family and friends, then you may be on your way to becoming a professional fashion designer one day!

Besides serving practical purposes in our everyday lives, our outfits also reflect our individual styles, tastes, and preferences. Fashion is a great vehicle for expressing ourselves in a unique and creative manner!

It is likely that the earliest clothing worn by our ancestors was used to cover their bodies and protect them from the elements. These were probably made of materials like fur, leather, leaves, and grass. Dyed plant fibres that may have been used as clothing were once found in a prehistoric cave in Georgia dating back to 34,000 BC. We can only guess at how our early ancestors used to dress since these natural materials would have deteriorated quite rapidly and not survive in the same way as hardier artefacts made from stone or metal.

However, did you know that archaeologists also discovered a sewing needle made of bird bone dating back to at least 50,000 years ago in Siberia? This needle belonged to a prehistoric human race from the Palaeolithic era and could be the first evidence of a man-made apparel-weaving tool!
Sewing needles made from ivory, copper, and iron have also been found in archaeological sites in Egypt, China, Australia, and parts of Western and Eastern Europe.

Over the ages, what we wear and how we style ourselves not only fulfil practical functions but also serve as aesthetic displays. Our ancestors used to wear jewellery, possibly to beautify themselves or communicate their wealth and status! The oldest known jewellery has been identified as a set of 150,000-year-old snail-shell beads discovered in Morocco. Each bead had a hole drilled through it, possibly to string them together so they could be worn as earrings or a necklace.

These ancient beads, similar to others discovered across the African continent, had polished edges, which suggest the skills and intentional effort of early craftspeople. Many traditional African accessories were also created from ivory husks, ostrich eggshells, carved wood or stone, and even porcupine quill! Early forms of jewellery may have been worn for ritual purposes, too, serving as protective amulets or religious symbols.

Besides emphasising what is beautiful and socially desirable, fashion is also a form of cultural expression. The way an attire was designed and how early humans donned it conveyed who they were, what they represented, and what was important or respected in their culture. In ancient Egypt, pharaohs used to wear royal headgear known as nemes. These were striped linen headcloths, some with the image of a cobra's rearing head at the top of the headdress. The cobra was a symbol of power and protection associated with Egyptian royalty, so we could definitely tell from the fashion who was king or queen back then!

Different kinds of attire and adornments in everyday wear also revealed different classes in early society. Ancient Egyptian civilisation saw working-class men wearing loincloths or short kilts while wealthier men wore long shirt-like garments tied with a sash at the waist. Female servants wore simple sheath dresses, while noblewomen wore more elaborate gowns, often enhancing their appearance with make-up, jewellery, wigs and hair ornaments too. A common clothing material used back then in the hot climate was linen made from the flax plant. And as for ancient Egyptian children, it was common for them to go without clothes until the age of six!

In highly class-structured societies such as the Zhou Dynasty in China, dressing as a symbol of social roles and status became especially pronounced. Distinctions in clothing colour, materials, patterns, and dress adornments were strictly established across all strata amongst the royal family, government officials, and common people. During this time, the colour yellow also became associated with the emperor. Over time, imperial yellow became so guarded in pre-modern China that anyone else seen wearing this colour was deemed a rebel and subject to punishment of death!

Fashion-wise, the early Chinese also discovered silk production around 3,000 BC. Legend has it that Empress Leizu was sipping tea beneath a mulberry tree when a silkworm cocoon fell into her teacup. Upon fishing it out, the cocoon began to unravel… leading to the beginnings of silk cultivation - a closely guarded secret for centuries in China! To this day, silk is considered a luxury item due to its soft and elegant texture. Did you know no single silk fibre is uniform, which explains its lively quality? Silk can also absorb dye like no other fabric, making it truly a fashion designer's playground!

The spread of silk cultivation and trade routes along the Silk Road had a significant influence on clothing design, textiles, and the art of embroidery. It brought together Middle Eastern, European, Chinese, and Far Eastern traders, resulting in the exchange of ideas and techniques. One such example is the intricate embroidery techniques that originated in India and were further developed during the Mughal period, incorporating silk with precious materials like gold and silver threads to create exquisite patterns.

These intricately woven fabrics provide the beautiful canvas to a variety of traditional Indian garments worn to this day, such as women's saris (a form of long draped robe), blouses, men's tunics, and wrapped trousers, to name just a few!

And wait till you see the type of shoes that came around during the Middle Ages in Europe. Back in those times, it was fashionable to wear shoes with such extremely long toes that the tips had to be tied with strings or chains to the wearer's knee to prevent the person from falling over when walking! These long-tipped shoes, worn mostly by men, were called poulaines and were meant to show off a person's wealth.

Not only were these shoes exorbitantly priced, they also made it impossible for you to perform manual labour while wearing these shoes, showing that you lived a life of leisure. (Poulains were ultimately banned because they made it hard for the wearer to kneel in prayer too!)

Another distinct fashion piece that arose later during the Renaissance period was the ruff collar. Also known as a millstone collar because it resembled the circular stones for grinding grain, ruffs were reserved only for the upper classes. The stiffness of a ruff forced an upright posture on the wearer, and at its height, a ruff could measure more than a metre wide! Called cartwheel ruffs, these had to be propped up with a wireframe to secure them at a fashionable angle. Ruffs were usually white or light-coloured, and, like poulaines, their apparent impracticality was part of showcasing the wearer's wealth and position in society.

Social status and etiquette were also defining expressions of clothing styles during the Victorian era (1837 - 1901). Women's dresses were made of heavy fabrics, with full skirts, tight corsets, and high necklines, all to emphasise a formal and respectable appearance. It was also customary to adorn a slew of accessories like gloves, bonnets, and expensive jewellery or be seen with a parasol (light umbrella) or an elaborately designed fan on hand. Men's clothing focussed on propriety, too, with suits, tailcoats, and top hats being common everyday attire for the well-to-do and accessories like pipes or watches to convey gentility.

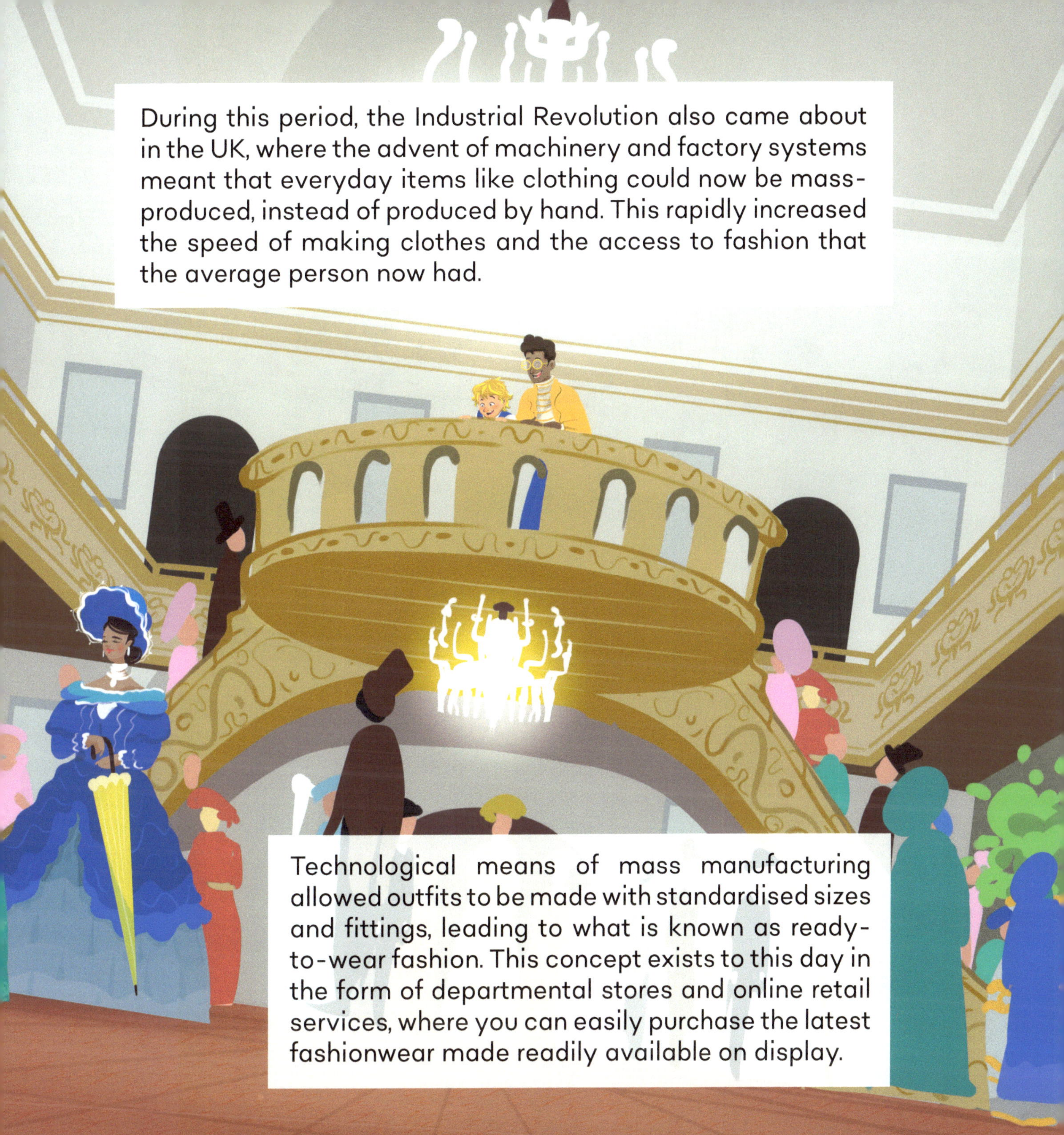

During this period, the Industrial Revolution also came about in the UK, where the advent of machinery and factory systems meant that everyday items like clothing could now be mass-produced, instead of produced by hand. This rapidly increased the speed of making clothes and the access to fashion that the average person now had.

Technological means of mass manufacturing allowed outfits to be made with standardised sizes and fittings, leading to what is known as ready-to-wear fashion. This concept exists to this day in the form of departmental stores and online retail services, where you can easily purchase the latest fashionwear made readily available on display.

Of course, the Industrial Revolution by no means put an end to exclusive and customised high fashion creations! Haute couture, literally translated as 'high sewing' from the French and founded by English designer Charles Frederick Worth in Paris during the mid-1800s, offered high-quality, custom-fitted dresses handmade from start to end.

Paris soon became the centre for haute couture, an exclusive arena catered to wealthy high society, where dresses were made with expensive and sometimes unusual materials by some of the most experienced sewers of the day with the greatest attention to detail.

While haute couture represents prestige and exclusivity, many early practices, such as designing seasonal collections that were then presented on live models at fashion shows, have directly influenced the catwalk or runway fashion practice of our present times.

Famous fashion brands continue to showcase their designs, often as ready-to-wear fashion, at seasonal shows across the world. These events are often eclectically designed to bring out the themes of that season's clothing collection. Some shows have also been held in unconventional settings, such as medieval castles and even in front of the Great Pyramids of Giza!

So what does it take to be a fashion designer in our world today? What skills and capacities might you need to thrive as a fashion expert? Well, for starters, it certainly helps if you love to make people feel good about themselves! Whether in everyday grooming techniques or dressing up for a special occasion, our outfits and accessories have the ability to uplift our mood, strengthen our confidence, and enhance our comfort in any situation.

She has been credited for transforming the face of women's fashion by breaking away from stiff corseted dressing conventions in the West and popularising a casual and sporty but no less chic style for the modern feminine. Chanel was also a prolific designer, creating jewellery, handbags, and her signature Chanel No. 5 perfume. As testimony to her groundbreaking and liberating contributions to fashion, she was the only fashion designer to be featured in Time magazine's Top 100 Most Influential People of the 20th Century!

As a fashion designer, you will also need to be knowledgeable about various clothing materials, textiles, and fabrics - how they interact with one another, what kinds of outfits they can be best used for, and how to bring out these myriad textual possibilities in your designs. I mean, we wouldn't want a presumably waterproof raincoat to be made of cotton or supposedly breathable undergarments to be made from plastic! (Unless you are planning to make a controversial fashion statement of course!) Either way, knowing your materials as a designer is certainly important indeed.

Did you know that one English designer invented his own fabric? Thomas Burberry created gabardine - a breathable and waterproof highly durable material that revolutionised rainwear for the world!

Up to then, rain-repellent apparel tended to be thick and heavy, but with Burberry's lightweight innovation opened up the possibilities of fashion with functionality. What's interesting is that Burberry founded his fashion line at just 21 years old on the basis that clothing should be designed to protect people from British weather! This led to his designs being donned by explorers and even military personnel who needed to brave harsh weather conditions in their missions.

So, being an innovative and
original thinker can certainly
go towards empowering your
fashion designs for your wearers,
possibly even for generations to come!
In more recent times, during the 21st century,
Japanese fashion designer Issey Miyake became
one such renowned avant-garde icon for his technology-
driven and even ergonomically-crafted fluid clothing design. Known for
collaborating with engineers and scientists to develop new methods in
fabric dyeing and textile pleating, Miyake also championed sustainable,
eco-friendly fashion that focussed on recycling and upcycling materials

If being creative, experimental, and even daring in your endeavours speaks to your heart, then you may just have what it takes to be a trailblazing fashion designer! Oftentimes, fashion experts also work with other professionals in the music, performing arts, and movie industries to design iconic looks in clothing, accessories, and even hairstyles, that can literally take the world by storm! Some designers also incorporate historical or cultural influences from the past to invigorate current-day fashionwear with a renewed spin. So the possibilities of expressing yourself in wearable styles are truly neverending!

Now, what are some of the actual steps you will need to take towards becoming a professional fashion designer? One way is to enrol in a fashion design degree where you can undertake formal study in the various aspects of clothing design, such as fabrics, colour theory, and fashion theory. You will also learn how to use design software to illustrate and visualise your fashion concepts.

Depending on what areas of fashion you specialise in, a degree of study could also entail learning about garment construction, merchandising practices, consumer lifestyles, branding, and other areas related to the fashion world.

Many of these fashion degrees also include internships where you move on to cultivate hands-on experience working for a professional fashion designer or company. This gives you the opportunity to build your portfolio while acquiring skills such as communication, presentation, research, teamwork, and marketing. Being adept at promoting your work is crucial when it comes to thriving in the field of fashion because, whether you choose to be self-employed or work for someone else, promotional and marketing expertise goes towards getting your design into retail establishments where your target consumers can purchase your pieces.

And in case you were wondering, yes, you can even be a self-taught fashion designer! How about taking a course in basic sewing techniques, to begin with? There are also online courses to understand fashion history and sustainable practices or short programmes in related areas such as lifestyle blogging or fashion photography.

There are also a variety of different jobs in the fashion industry that you can explore as part of your journey towards being a fashion designer.

Fashion consultants help to create specific looks for their clients by styling their clothing, makeup, accessories, and hair.

Fashion writers cover the latest trends and events in magazines or online blogs to inform fashion enthusiasts. Fashion merchandisers select, purchase, and plan displays for products to attract buyers at a retail store. And fashion marketers design campaigns to promote the latest wearable styles and aesthetics.

With the increasing use of technology like social media platforms and the internet, fashion and its possibilities have certainly vastly evolved from its early days amongst our ancestors! Nowadays, we can easily see what celebrities, influencers, and even the everyday person are wearing and how they groom themselves. People can also easily set up their own businesses these days to sell their fashion merchandise online, often as simple as opening a social media account to promote their brand.

If this excites you at all and is beginning to spark the creative juices in your mind, what fashion apparel or outfits do you see yourself designing? Colourful socks for the quirky fashionista? High-fashion luxury scarves for both women and men? Or maybe futuristic sportswear that enhances our physical performance with style and flair!

GRANDE PREMIERE
FASHION WEEK
DESIGNER:
Fashion expands the reaches of not only our creativity and aesthetic expression but also pushes the innovative edge of what is yet humanly possible in the way we move and carry out our everyday activities. Would you be our next fashion iconoclast?

My Inspiration

Shubhi Saxena
Founder, Unibino

As a parent in this ever-changing world, it can sometimes feel overwhelming when it comes to our children's futures. New technologies seem to be arising almost every day, and with so many innovations, it creates unique professions which many of us wouldn't have dreamed to be necessary only a few years ago. Which to me is a good thing. Because with so much variety, my children can have the opportunity to pick a career that will fit their personalities and build upon their strengths. As you may imagine, this desire within me to provide my children with the resources they needed to thrive, led me to search out books that would be easy enough for them to understand while teaching them about various professions.

Only, I found that these books were few and far between. Even if I could find a book about a certain profession geared towards young readers, I found them sparse inside and limited to only certain careers that may not fit my children's abilities. This is when I came up with the idea to write my own children's books, teaching them about all the various careers in the modern world. After months of researching different professions and learning more than I ever expected, I quickly realised this was going to be a bigger project than I first anticipated. I dove into the histories of these professions, discovering links to the past, and why these professions were now so important.

Ultimately my goal was to offer my children options, to show them that there is no one set path for everyone. But in this, I stumbled upon something bigger. I wanted to share this with future generations. To share with all children and parents about these careers, to help spark curiosity, and to instil a passion for the future. Everyone has special talents and abilities, and I hope that this series will be able to offer clarity and inspiration to children around the world. Because at the end of the day, it's never too early to start dreaming and never too late to take action. With this, I hope you enjoy this series and that your young ones become the best versions of themselves as they can achieve.